Alba's Abruzzo

Alba's Abruzzo

Recipes from the Heart of Italy

Rock DiLisio

ALBA'S ABRUZZO
RECIPES FROM THE HEART OF ITALY

Editor: Erica M. Hollabaugh

iUniverse books may be ordered through booksellers or by contacting:

iUniverse
1663 Liberty Drive
Bloomington, IN 47403
www.iuniverse.com
1-800-Authors (1-800-288-4677)

ISBN: 978-1-5320-1938-8 (sc)
ISBN: 978-1-5320-1939-5 (e)

Print information available on the last page.

iUniverse rev. date: 03/16/2017

Chapter One

Alba and Abruzzo

The youngest of nine children, Alba (DiGenova) DiLisio was born in Sulmona, Italy in the province of Abruzzo. Her parents, Cosimo and Lucia DiGenova, and her elder brothers and sisters-Elena. Olga, Aldo, Tullio, Ezio, Dora, Angelo and Guido – were also born in Sulmona.

Sulmona sits in the heart of Abruzzo and is an ancient, bustling city of 25,000 people. No truer Italian cuisine can be found in Italy than in this east central province. This is where Alba learned the art of Italian cooking and enhanced the time-honored recipes of the past, which were primarily passed on to her by her mother and sisters. Alba took that tutelage to another level and eventually to the United States.

After her marriage to Angelo DiLisio (also of Sulmona) in 1959, Alba moved to Coraopolis, Pennsylvania, a suburb of Pittsburgh. This is where she had her two children, Maria and Rocky, and her culinary expertise became well known. Alba's house was always the place to go for excellent meals and decadent desserts. She had a flair for making the ordinary extraordinary, all in the atmosphere of where you felt welcomed. This book brings you the recipes that she uses and that have garnered her the reputation of a true Italian cook...from the true part of Italy...Abruzzo. Buon Appetito!

As Alba says:

"Volete mangiare bene, mangia Abruzzese"

(If you want to eat well, eat Abruzzi cuisine)

Abruzzo – The True Italy

The Italy of one's imagination is envisioned as one encompassing the numerous tourist meccas, which have delighted and entertained countless visitors over the past century. The cities of Rome, Florence, Venice, Milan and Naples are recognized by even the least of worldly travelers, and the same can be said of the famous regions, such as Tuscany and Lombardia. Italy simply has a vast array of cultural and topographical locations to enthrall and tantalize even the most skeptical of travelers. After all, it's not often that you encounter someone who did not enjoy their visit to *Italia*.

If someone where to ask, "Where can I go to see the *true* Italy?" – What would be the response? This is a difficult question to answer, because even near the tourist meccas sit smaller locales that are seemingly unscathed by the throng of travelers. Life goes on there, as it has for millennia and it will continue too. The typical answer to the question, though, would be the Province of Abruzzo.

This is not at all surprising considering that the name "Italia" or "Italy" originated in Abruzzo. *"The name Italia was imposed upon the Roman Republic by the conquering Italic tribes of the contemporary Abruzzo region, centering in the area of Corfinium (Corfinio)."*

Abruzzo is located in east/central Italy and is approximately 50 miles due east from Rome. The Adriatic Sea to the east, and the Apennine Mountains to its west primarily border it. Abruzzo also borders the region of Marche to the north, Molise to the south-east and Lazio to the west. Without question, Abruzzo is located in one of the most mountainous regions in all of Italy. The Apennines includes the tallest peak on the Italian peninsula, the Gran Sasso, and Europe's southernmost glacier, the Calderone.

The winding Apennine mountain range is what creates the imposing physical, and yet imaginary border between the Italy we all know and the Italy we truly want to experience. Nestled on the eastern side of the Apennines is the region of Abruzzo, seemingly forgotten by the average tourist. While in Italy, tourists often seek the major cities and regions of known popularity, neither of which Abruzzo offers in abundance. Though this is the case, this happenstance has now evolved into a tourist destination of a different sort.

The Abruzzo region is considered by many to be remote and mountainous. The Apennines have been an obstacle for travelers not wanting to drive the high, winding mountainous roads, which are the primary, and sometimes the only, entry points to the province. Travelers have skirted the region for centuries in search of smoother lanes of travel, which they find in abundance.

The isolation of the region, though, is now considered by many to be "God's Country," where you can find some of the least visited cities and hill towns in all of Italy. This is why Abruzzo is considered the "True Italy," where the average Italian toils in his/her daily life, where old-world traditions still reign, all without the overwhelming monetary influence of the tourist. Though tourism has increased over the years, Abruzzo is still an area visited primarily by other Italians and various Europeans. The interest in Abruzzo steadily increases with each passing year, as tourists are attracted to the region for its rich cluster of castles and its medieval heritage towns. Over the past decades, tourism in Abruzzo has increased, again primarily among Italians and other Europeans. Abruzzo's wealth of castles and medieval towns has led it to be called by the nickname of "Abruzzoshire" by many. This nickname is a reference to the analogy with the "Chiantishire" nickname, often used to refer to the Chianti area of Tuscany. Still, even with the increased influx of tourism, Abruzzo is still off the beaten path for most visitors to Italy.

Whether you like the seashore or the mountains, river valleys or ancient towns, Abruzzo has something pleasing for everyone and is a region rich of work and passion, of history and where life is sometimes as untouched and golden as it was in centuries past.

Chapter Two

The Foods of Abruzzo

The Abruzzo region is also known for a number of unique, regional products. The gastronomic culture of Abruzzo is made up in large part by the influences of the surrounding regions. There is still an abundance of sheep farming and agriculture throughout the region and those products are used to create some of the most traditional meals in all of Italy. The Abruzzese cuisine is not only traditional and simple, but also delicious and made with genuine Italian ingredients. From the aromatic Abruzzo olive oil to excellent truffles, this is home cooking Italian style. Abruzzo's food is not flashy, but very simple and generally inexpensive. During times of celebration, the cooks of Abruzzo become more elaborate.

The mountains in Abruzzo are also full of small and ancient towns that have a very unique, but also a simple gastronomy characterized by different basic ingredients. The cuisines of Abruzzo are divided into basically two parts-the mountains and the sea, and you will find many unique Italian recipes not found elsewhere.

Pasta Region

Abruzzo is home to one of the Italian capitals of pasta production, namely Fara San Martino, which is a small town at the foot of the Majella. Since ancient times there have been three specialized manufacturers that now export all over the world. These manufacturers include: Cavalier Cocco, De Cecco, and Del Verde.

The region is also famous for certain types of pasta, in particular what is known as *maccheroni alla chitarra* (loosely translated as *Guitar String Pasta*). The name comes from the fact that maccheroni are prepared using a real string instrument consisting of a rectangular wooden frame on which are fixed some very thin steel strings – resembling guitar strings. Abruzzo is famous for its excellent dried pasta, the best of which is made by local artisans. This traditional first-course Abruzzo pasta is often covered with marinara sauce made from locally grown tomatoes or tomatoes with basil sauce.

The Abruzzo Table

The meats include locally made sausage and farm raised pork, lamb, duck and goose. Breeding is a main activity in Abruzzo, which makes the meat the most important ingredient in all of the regional recipes. One of the most well known dishes of Abruzzo is lamb. In particular, lamb boiled in water and containing little to no flavoring, but still produces a flavorful dish. This system of cooking originates from the early days of the region when shepherds needed a quick means of preparation. Lamb is also often prepared using a recipe called *Cacio e uova*, meaning with pecorino cheese and egg. There is also Arrosticini, which are thin mutton skewers grilled over charcoal (kebab). Lamb is very famous in the mountains and thus is the favorite dish there. It has consequently overtaken mutton and is kept reserved for special occasions.

Pork is another widely used traditional meat dish in Abruzzo. The processing of pork, another widespread activity in the region, has lead to the creation of a great selection of hams, sausages, and salamis. One popular selection is the traditional liver sausage, which is often preserved in oil. Other traditional products include: Soppressate, smoked ham, mortadella. One of the more well-known pork dishes is often called *'ndocca*, which is a stew of boiled pork.

When taking into account fresh sausage a mention has to be made of the pork liver mortadella, which is unique unto itself. In this type of sausage you may encounter two types: Liver sweetened with honey and the likes of candied fruits and even cedar – this is known as "sweet liver." The other replaces honey with chilly peppers in the recipe. Another well regarded meat dish in Abruzzo is crespelle, which is a flavorful Italian crepe, stuffed and cooked in the oven with meat sauce or on the stovetop in a simmering broth.

Fish and Seafood Dishes

The fish and seafood dishes are usually more elaborate than their meat counterparts. The coastal cooking is obviously fish-based. Some of the more well known dishes are fish-soups from Adriatic coastal towns such as Pescara, Vasto and San Vito. These dishes are better known as *brodetti* and this dish recipe is often changed based on what section of Abruzzo it comes from. In some locations, the brodetti is made with a much stronger flavor involving chilly peppers and tomatoes. Overall, the recipes tend to rely less on tomato and more on pepperoncino, especially in the fish stews. The other main Abruzzo seafood meals encompass great mussels, shellfish, bluefish and rock fish and are typically served with pasta, risotto, salad and soups. Other coastal fish dishes of note include cod, sole, anchovies, prawns and cuttlefish.

Cheeses

Cheese and Italy are sometimes synonymous. Sheep farming is the most common form of animal farming in Abruzzo, which explains its importance in the role of regional cooking. Sheep's milk cheese is prominent in Abruzzo's dairy production.

The cheese from Abruzzo farms, such as Burrelle (butter filled), Caciocavallo (a bigger form of dried mozzarella), Caciottta (cow's and sheep's milk) and Scamorza (dried mozzarella-young and aged) are known to be excellent. There is also Pecorino (ewe's milk cheese, either fresh or seasoned) and sheep ricotta, as well as excellent dairy products, such as trecce (platted), bocconcini (very small fresh mozzarella), and fiordilatte (small fresh mozzarella) all produced in Abruzzo and surrounding areas.

From the Farm

Truffles are a well-known product of the Abruzzo region and there are as many as 28 truffle varieties. The black truffle (tartufo nero) is the best known and most widely used. The truffle heavily influences many dishes, in particular, white sauces used on pasta. The locals and their truffle-sniffing dog typically find truffles, though pigs are sometimes also used. The delicacy is a prominent industry in the region.

Another typical ingredient of this zone is the red garlic of Sulmona. This garlic is covered in a wine red skin with white cloves and is larger than normal in size. Just before harvesting, the garlic is more floral, often referred to as producing the *"zolla."*

Other interesting products grown in Abruzzo include Santo Stefano di Sessanio lentils, which are flat and dark brown in color. This iron rich legume has a nice taste and supposedly has its historical origins originating from the Middle Ages – possibly arriving from Turkey. Cicerchia, or grass-pea, is a regional specialty and the likes of *diavolillo peperoncino* is used to flavor just about any dish. There is also an enormous selection of fresh farm vegetables.

As with any great meal, the spices and various added flavorings create the unique regional taste. One such prominent Abruzzo spice is saffron. Saffron comes from the tiny, colorful Crocus flower, which blooms in late winter to early spring. The Province of L'Aquila produces very high quality saffron with a potent and great taste. The L'Aquila saffron is so highly regarded that it is shipped across the world and it is one of the few places in the world where it is farmed.

Abruzzo is also a big producer of extra virgin olive oil and the region has three classified varieties. The extra-virgin olive oil of Abruzzo is often considered just as good as any of the best Italian oils. Though it is a very important commercial industry in the area, much production still comes from family-operated businesses. During November and December, families are also known to spend weekends picking their olives and taking them to the local mill press for personal olive oil production.

Freshly picked fruit is a traditional way to complete any Italian meal. Many types of fruit are grown in Abruzzo, including cherries, walnuts, figs, strawberries, plums, and, of course, grapes. The most famous of the grape varieties are the Montepulciano grapes, which are small, black grapes that are made into the prestigious Montepulciano d'Abruzzo wine.

Beekeepers produce excellent and delicious tasting honey all across Abruzzo. The jelly and honeys are well regarded.

Dessert

For dessert, the famous pizzelles (wafers/waffles) are most popular, but so are bocconotti (small pastry-nut filled with dried fruit and cocoa – best known from Castel Frentano). The traditional Biscotti are always available, as are the Torrones (soft nougat candy) and the world-famous Abruzzo (Sulmona) Confetti (sugared almonds). Sulmona is considered the world-capital of *confetti*, also known as Jordan or sugared almonds. The other types of confetti are filled with liquor and jellies. Other traditional sweet pastries of Abruzzo are mostaccioli (chocolate covered nut biscuit), and cicerchiata (pastry balls stuck together with honey).

Wines/Beverages

Abruzzo is also known as a good region for grape growing. Abruzzo is considered to be the fifth largest producer of wine globally and has Italy's highest average yield for bulk wines (at 110 million gallons)-per various sources. Since it is mostly a mountainous and hilly region, it is perfect for growing grapevines with the most common grapes grown in the region being Montepulciano and Trebbiano, though the wineries are working to produce more varieties.

The Montepulciano and Tebbiano grapes produce excellent soft red wines with full, rich and robust flavors. Abruzzo is primarily known for the red Montepulciano d'Abruzzo variety. This robust and strong wine is also produced in the Montelpulciano d'Abruzzo Colline Teramane variety. Montepulciano wines brands that have been found abroad include the brands Dragani and Citra. The other primary produced wines of the region are Trebbiano d'Abruzzo (red), Trebbiano d'Abruzzo (white), Contro Guerra and the red Cerasuolo. All of these wines are excellent and beginning to obtain international recognition. The wines of the region are ideally suitable with red meat and aged cheeses.

The many Abruzzo-made liqueurs include chocolate, coffee, cherry, strawberry and blueberry. The Pescara area is most famous for liqueurs such as, Centerba (100 grasses), which has a unique taste and a vivid green color and Aurum, which is orange flavored liquor. Many of these beverages are over 40 percent proof or have even a higher alcohol content.

Chapter Three

Alba's Real Italian Recipes

Main Dishes

Meats

Abruzzo Chicken

- 2 pounds of diced, boneless chicken breasts
- 8 pieces of cleaned garlic
- 1 tsp. of salt/pepper – add to taste
- 1 cup Balsamic vinegar
- ½ cup of olive oil

Marinate chicken in Balsamic vinegar, oil and salt/pepper for one hour. Add olive oil and garlic to frying pan. Sautee until garlic is golden. Add chicken and salt/pepper to taste. Sautee until chicken is cooked – up to one-hour.

Chicken Cacciatore

- 4 boneless, skinless chicken breast halves
- 1 16 oz. Jar of spaghetti sauce
- 1 can of tomatoes – chopped and drained
- 1 large onion – chopped
- 1/8 tsp. pepper
- 1 large green bell pepper – cut into strips
- 8 oz. Of whole wheat spaghetti (cooked)

Spray 10-inch skillet with non-stick cooking spray. Add chicken and cook over medium heat for 3 minutes – each side. Add spaghetti sauce, tomatoes, onion and pepper. Bring ingredients to a boil. Reduce to medium and add in pepper. Allow to simmer until ingredients are cooked. Chicken should be served over cooked spaghetti.

Parmigiano Wings

- 20 wings
- 1 ½ tbsp. Of Salt
- 1 tsp. Of Pepper
- 3 cups of flour
- ½ tsp. Of garlic powder
- 3 or 4 cups of wing sauce of choice (mild is typically used)
- 1 cup of parmigiano cheese

Salt and pepper wings and then flour them. Place on cookie sheet and bake at 450 degrees for 1 and ½ hours. Prepare sauce by adding garlic powder to sauce and butter. Once wings are cooked, brush with sauce mixture and then sprinkle with cheese. Place wings in oven for 15 – 20 minutes or to taste.

Breaded Fettine (Meat)

- 6 Thin Breakfast Steaks
- 2 cups of flour
- 2 eggs
- 2 cups of bread crumbs
- Salt and Pepper
- Romano Cheese
- Parsley
- Oregano
- Olive oil

Salt and pepper the steaks. Add flour, breadcrumbs and eggs into separate bowls – one ingredient in each bowl. Add a little salt, pepper, Romano cheese, chopped parsley and oregano to eggs and mix. Dust steaks with flour, dip steaks into eggs and then bread with breadcrumbs. Place steaks into frying pan with olive oil and golden both sides. Place steaks on baking sheet, place into oven at 350 degrees for ½ hour.

Osso Bucco

- 6 pieces of chuck roast (beef)
- 2 carrots
- 4 stocks of celery
- 1 onion
- Salt and Pepper
- 1 quart of chicken stock

Portion pieces for six people. Salt & Pepper to taste. Dust beef with flour. Place pieces in frying pan with olive oil and golden both side of beef.

Place pieces into a casserole. Chop celery, carrots and onion and sauté. Place vegetables on top of meat. Add chicken stock to casserole until meat is covered. Cover with lid or aluminum foil. Place in oven at 400 degrees for 2 hours. Check meat for tenderness. If not tender, cook until tender. Remove from oven and let stand for 15 minutes.

Italian Meatballs

- 1 pd. Ground meat
- 1 cup of bread crumbs
- 2 eggs
- Add to taste – garlic, salt, pepper, oregano
- ½ cup Romano cheese

Mix all ingredients together. Make meatballs. Brown in oven or frying pan.

Italian Party Meatballs

- 1 cup of Corn Flakes
- 2 lbs. of hamburger
- 2 tbsp. onion Flakes
- 2 tbsp. soy sauce
- ¼ tsp. black pepper

- ½ tsp. garlic powder
- 2 eggs
- ½ cup ketchup

Mix ingredients together and roll into firm meatballs (1 to 1 ½ inch). Choose your favorite flavoring sauce and pour over meatballs. Bake 35-40 minutes at 400 degrees.

Italian Sausage

- 2 pds. Italian sausage
- 1 jar of marinara sauce
- 2 green peppers
- 2 onions (medium)
- Salt and pepper

Boil sausage for ½ hour. Chop pepper and onions and sauté in frying pan using salt and pepper. Remove sausage from boil and cut into 3 inch pieces. Place sausage, pepper/onions and marinara sauce into a pot. Allow to cook for one hour.

Pasta

Fettucine Alfredo

- ½ pd. Pasta (cooked al dente)
- ½ stick of butter
- 1 cup of heavy cream
- 1 cup of grated parmigiano cheese

Mix butter, heavy cream and cheese (sauté). Boil pasta al dente. Lay Alfredo sauce on pasta.

Gnocchi

- 4 lbs of peeled potatoes (peeled)
- 3 lbs. Of all-purpose flour
- 3 lbs. Of semolina (flour)
- 3 eggs
- 4 tbsp. of salt

Makes 8 pounds. Blend ingredients and make dough. Pull pieces of dough and roll into one-inch think portions. Cut one-inch pieces. Bring water to boil, add salt, add gnocchi. Bring to second boil. When gnocchi rises to the top, allow pasta to boil for five more minutes and then remove. Add sauce and cheese and serve.

Lasagna

- 1 pound of lasagna pasta (Uncooked – store bought)
- 2 pounds of ground meat
- 1 pound of mozzarella cheese shredded
- 1 pound of parmigiano grated
- 1 ½ quarts of pasta sauce

Lay pasta at bottom of casserole-add meat, cheeses and sauce. Another layer of pasta and repeat. Another layer of pasta and repeat. Add a final layer of pasta on top, add sauce and cheese. Bake at 400 degrees for approximately one-hour. Makes one 9x13 pan.

Macaroni and Cheese

- Elbow pasta
- 3 cups of milk
- 4 tbsp. of butter
- 3 tbsp. of flour
- 1 tsp. of salt

- 1 cup of cheese
- 1 cup of cream

Mix all ingredients. Boil pasta (elbow) and add the mixture. Add some cheese and butter on top, if you wish. Place in oven for 15 minutes and then serve.

Sides

Zucchini Quiche

- 2 cups zucchini – cut
- 1 onion – cut
- 1 cup of Bisquick
- 4 eggs
- ½ cup vegetable oil
- ½ cup of parmesan cheese
- ½ tsp. black pepper
- parsley – to taste

Beat eggs in large bowl and add oil, Bisquick – mix well. Add zucchini, onion, cheese, parsley and pepper. Still until zucchini is well coated. Pour into a buttered pie plate or quiche pan. Bake at 350 degrees for 30 minutes.

Roasted Peppers

- 10 peppers (sliced)
- 2 sliced onions
- 1 garlic
- 4 tomatoes
- Salt and Pepper to taste

Cover in roaster with oil. Cook in oven at 350 degrees for 1½ hours.

Broccoli and Rice Casserole

- 2 – 10 oz. packages of frozen broccoli cuts
- 1 – 8 oz. Jars of Cheese Wiz
- 1 can of cream of chicken soup
- 1 can of cream of mushroom soup

- 1 cup of milk
- 2 sticks of butter
- 2 small onions
- 2 cups of Minute Rice

Sauté onions in butter. Add broccoli, cheese, rice, soup, milk and onion together. Bake in a 9x13 glass dish at 350 degrees for 1 hour.

Italian Risotto

- 5 tbsp. extra virgin olive oil
- 6 cups chicken broth
- 1 medium onion – chopped
- 2 ½ cups Arborio rice
- ¾ cup of white wine
- ½ tsp. Saffron powder
- ½ cup parmesan cheese
- Salt to taste

Sauté onion in olive oil – until soft. Add in rice and fully coat. Add wine and stir over medium heat until wine evaporates. Add some broth to cover ingredients and stir until liquid is absorbed. Add more broth slowly while stirring. Dissolve saffron in hot broth and then add it to the rice mixture. Stir in cheese and then season to taste with salt. Best when served immediately.

Pasta Salad

- 1 pd. Linguine pasta (chopped and cooked)
- 1 16 oz. Bottle of Italian dressing
- ½ bottle of McCormick Salad Supreme
- 1 small onion (chopped)
- 1 green pepper (chopped)
- 1 tomato (seeded and chopped)
- 1 cucumber (seeded and chopped)

Mix together and chill for up to 12 to 24 hours.

Breaded Cauliflower

- 1 head of cauliflower
- 2 cups of flour
- 2 eggs
- 2 cups of bread crumbs
- Salt & Pepper
- Romano Cheese
- Parsley
- Oregano
- Olive Oil

Cut cauliflower into pieces (small heads). Blanche for a couple of minutes. Salt and Pepper to taste. Add flour, breadcrumbs and eggs to separate bowls-one ingredient in each bowl. In eggs, add a little salt, pepper, parsley, oregano and Romano cheese. Dust cauliflower with flour; dip them into the eggs and then bread. Place into a deep fryer until golden. You can also sauté if no deep fryer is available

Zucchini Puffs

- 3 grated zucchini
- 3 eggs
- 2 cups of flour
- ½ cup Romano cheese
- ½ cup of bread crumbs
- 2 tsp. of baking powder
- Salt/pepper/parsley/garlic to taste

Mix all ingredients and drop teaspoonful size pieces into hot oil. Cook/remove and serve.

Soups, Breads and More

Minestrone Soup

- 1 pound of tubettini pasta
- 4 potatoes (diced)
- 1 can of white or red beans
- 1 cup of celery (diced)
- 1 large can of chicken soup
- 1 cup of pasta sauce
- 1 cup of Romano cheese
- 1 tsp. of salt
- 1 tsp. of pepper

Add chicken soup, pasta sauce, potatoes, celery and salt/pepper to pot (salt/pepper to taste). Allow potatoes to cook and then add pasta and beans. Allow pasta to cook. Add cheese and serve.

Italian Wedding Soup

- 1 bunch of endive (blanched and chopped)
- 1 pound of ground meat
- 2 eggs
- Bread crumbs
- Chicken Broth
- 1 garlic
- Parmesan cheese grated
- Salt and Pepper

Make small meatballs with ground meat. eggs, garlic and breadcrumbs. Place broth, meatballs and endive into pot. Boil for 15 minutes. Beat two eggs with Parmesan cheese and then add to soup while boiling. Remove heat.

Pizza Dough or Bread

- 5 cups of water
- 2 tbsp. of salt
- ½ cup of sugar
- 10 cups of flour
- 2 envelopes of yeast
- ½ cup of vegetable oil

Melt yeast in ¾ cups of water. Mix all ingredients and knead the dough. Cover and let rise for 2 hours. Place in bread or pizza pan. Bake the bread or pizza until golden brown at 400 degrees. If making pizza, add sauce, cheese and other toppings before baking.

Clover Leaf Rolls

- 2 cups of warm milk
- ¼ cup of butter
- ¼ cup of sugar
- 1 ½ tsp. of salt
- 2 envelopes of yeast
- 5 to 6 cups of flour

Mix ingredients together and knead into dough. Butter cup cake pan; place three small balls of dough into each cupcake hole. Let rise in pan until double in size. Bake at 375 degrees for 15-20 minutes or until gold. Once baked, brush with melted butter.

Pesto Sauce

- 1 cup of basil
- 1 cup of olive oil
- 1 cup of walnuts
- 1 tbsp. of garlic (ground)

- 1 cup of parmigiano cheese
- Salt and Pepper to taste.

Blend together and place on pasta.

Manicotti (filling)

- 1 ½ lb. Ricotta cheese
- 1 tsp. Pepper
- ¼ cup parsley
- 1 cup mozzarella
- 2 eggs

Mix all ingredients and lay individually on lasagna pasta dough (boil until soft if store purchased). Roll dough with filling. Line casserole with manicotti and place tomato sauce over manicotti. Sprinkle with parmigiano cheese and bake for ½ hour at 400 degrees.

Sweet Italian Dip

- 1 ½ cup of plain Greek yogurt
- 3 tbsp. of maple syrup
- ½ tsp. Of vanilla
- Pinch of salt

Cover and chill.

Pancake – Wrap – Manicotti Mix

For Wraps or Manicotti

- 1 cup of flour
- 1 cup of milk
- 3 eggs
- 1 pinch of salt
- 1 tbsp. of butter

For Pancakes

- Same ingredients above
- 5 tbsp. sugar
- Sprinkle of vanilla

Mix ingredients and make dough as you would pancakes. The Wrap and Manicotti dough would be made more thinly. Makes approximately 30 Wraps.

Desserts

Amaretti

- 2 ½ pounds of almond paste
- 2 cups of sugar
- 8 egg whites
- 1 tsp. almond extract

Beat egg whites until fluffy. Add sugar a little at a time – fold in almond paste and extract. Place dough in refrigerator for 10 minutes. Remove and make into cookie shape. Roll in sugar and then bake at 300 degrees for 20 minutes or golden brown. Makes 5 dozen.

Biscotti

- 4 eggs
- 1 tsp. Of almond extract
- 1 tbsp. of vanilla extract
- 1 cup of milk
- 3 whiskey glasses of baking powder
- ½ cup of Crisco (melted)
- 1/3 cup of vegetable oil
- 1 ½ cup of sugar
- 6 cups of flour

Mix ingredients into dough. Make into small balls and lay on cookie sheet. Bake at 350 degrees until golden.

Ceci Ripieni

Filling

- 4 cans of chick peas (boiled, drained and mashed)
- 30 oz. Of honey
- 1 Pound of roasted nuts (ground)
- 2 grated orange peels
- 2 grated lemons peels
- 1/3 box cocoa
- 1 tbsp. Cinnamon

Dough

- 8 cups flour
- 2 glasses of red wine (water glass size)
- 1 ¼ water glasses vegetable oil
- 4 tbsp. Sugar

Mix all ingredients. Roll dough and fill with one teaspoon of filling. (Ravioli size). Deep fry with Crisco (solid).

Ricotta Biscotti

- 2 cups sugar
- 2 sticks of butter
- 4 cups of flour
- 2 cups of ricotta cheese
- 5 tsp. of baking powder
- 4 eggs
- 2 tbsp. of vanilla

Mix all ingredients. Drop into greased cookie sheet by spoonful. Bake at 350 degrees until golden.

Nutella Cookies

Dough:

- 1-8 oz. Package of cream cheese
- ½ pound of butter
- 1 cup of flour

Mix all ingredients. Spread with rolling pin to ¼ inch thickness. Use small glass or dough cutter to cut out circles of dough.

Filling:

- 1 jar of Nutella

Add one teaspoon of Nutella to each piece of dough. Fold over and shape similar to ravioli. Bake 350 degrees for ½ hour or golden.

Scarponi

- 10 cups of flour
- 1 cup of cocoa
- 1 qt. Musto cotto (Boiled grape juice syrup)
- 1 pd. Of chopped and roasted walnuts or almonds
- 2 cups of sugar
- ½ pd. Crisco (melted) – 1 ½ cups
- 2 tbsp. of cinnamon
- 2 grated orange skins
- 3 tbsp. of baking powder
- 1 tsp. baking soda
- ½ cup of milk
- 1 tsp. Of lemon extract
- 1 tsp. Of vanilla extract

Mix all ingredients into a dough. Shape into round ball cookies – drop with tablespoon onto cookie sheet. Bake until golden at 350 degrees.

Gullets

- 1 lb. Of butter
- 2 ½ cups of sugar
- 2 tbsp. of Crisco (large)
- 8 eggs
- 8 cups of flour
- 2 tsp. Of baking powder
- 1 tsp. Of vanilla extract
- ½ bottle of almond extract (small)

Need a Gullet iron (looks like a small waffle iron). Mix ingredients into dough and drop a teaspoon or dough into the iron.

Easter Bread

- 30 cups of flour
- 3 dozen eggs
- 3 lbs of sugar
- 2 ½ pds. Crisco (melted and cooled)
- 1½ lbs. raisins (soak first)
- 1 ½ cups of milk (warm)
- 5 packages of yeast (melt in milk)
- 1 tsp. Of lemon, orange, vanilla and anise extracts
- Consider a little food coloring

Mix ingredients into dough and let rise until it doubles. Place dough into a bread pan. Brush loafs with beaten eggs. Heat oven to 250 degrees and bake 45 minutes to 1 hour.

Italian Apple Chips

- 2 apples
- ¼ cups of sugar
- 1 tsp. Of cinnamon
- ¼ tsp. Of salt

Slice apples and coat with ingredients. Place on cookie sheet. Heat oven to 300 degrees and bake for 40-45 minutes.

Ricotta Pie

Dough

- 6 eggs
- 1 cup of sugar
- 1 cup of Crisco
- 4 cups of flour
- 1 tbsp. of baking powder

Cream sugar and Crisco – beat in eggs one at a time.

Filling

- 6 eggs
- 3 tsp. Of vanilla
- 5 tbsp. sugar
- ¼ tsp. Of cinnamon
- ¼ cup of honey
- 4 pds. Of ricotta cheese

Mix cinnamon and sugar together, then add the remainder of the ingredients – then add ricotta. Bake at 350 degrees for 1 hour or until a toothpick comes out dry. Makes approximately 2 large pies.

Nutrolls

This is a double-recipe:

Dough

- 12 cups of flour
- 2 cups of Crisco
- 2 tsp. of salt
- 1 cup of sugar
- 2 cans of evaporated milk
- 6 egg yolks
- 2 tsp. of vanilla
- 1 cup of water (warm)
- 2 envelopes of yeast (melted in warm water)

Mix flour, Crisco and salt into piecrust dough. Then add other ingredients. Let rise for ½ hour.

Filling

- 4 pounds of walnuts (ground fine)
- 5 cups of sugar
- 2 cups or 1 lb. of melted butter
- 4 eggs (beaten)
- 3 cups of milk (evaporated) or 2 12oz cans
- ½ teaspoon of salt

Mix ingredients together and cook slowly on stovetop. Stir constantly for ½ hour.

Flatten dough, add filling, roll and bake for 45 minutes at 350 degrees. Before baking, brush rolled dough with egg wash.

____

Rock DiLisio

Alba's Specialties

Alba's specialties include Abruzzo Chicken and Osso Bucco as main dishes, Zucchini Puffs, Broccoli Cheese Casserole and Breaded Cauliflower as sides, Clover Leaf Rolls as bread and Gullets and Nut Rolls as dessert. Alba also makes homemade Concord wine.

Other Family Recipes

Chef Alba has passed her culinary cooking techniques onto family members who carry on the tradition in Abruzzo-style fashion. Here are some of their favorite recipes.

Maria Flasco – (Alba's Daughter)

Pasta Carbonara

- 1 lb. of bacon
- 1 lb. of spaghetti or linguine
- 4-5 large eggs
- ½ cup of Romano Cheese
- ½ tsp. of oregano
- ½ tsp. of dry basil
- 1 tsp. of chopped garlic
- Olive oil
- Pinch of salt and pepper

Chop bacon and sauté with garlic and olive oil. Beat eggs with cheese, oregano, basil, salt and pepper. Cook pasta reserving some water – place water in a serving bowl. Add pasta to pan with bacon and egg mixtures. Toss until egg is cooked. Place into pasta bowl, garnish with more cheese and fresh basil.

Chicken Cacciatore

- 7-8 Chicken legs or thighs
- 1 can of tomato sauce
- ½ cup of sliced mushrooms
- 1 green pepper sliced
- 1 tsp. of chopped garlic

- ½ tsp. of dry oregano
- Salt, pepper and olive oil

Sauté olive oil and garlic. Add peppers, tomato sauce, mushrooms and seasonings. Cook until vegetables are tender. Season chicken and place in a baking dish. Toss with tomatoes and vegetables. Bake at 400 degrees for 1 to 1 ½ hours or until chicken is done.

Chicken Picata

- 8-9 boneless chicken breasts (thin)
- 1 cup of flour
- 1 tbsp. of lemon zest
- 1 tsp. of garlic powder
- 1 cup of chicken broth
- ½ cup of white wine
- ½ cup of capers
- Olive oil, salt and pepper.

Salt and pepper chicken. Mix flour with lemon zest and flour chicken. Brown in pan with olive oil. Remove from pan and add broth and white wine. Simmer for up to 3 minutes. Return chicken to pan and add capers. Cook for approximately ½ hour to 40 minutes or until done.

Fettucino Alfredo

- ½ pound of fettucine pasta
- 1 cup of half & half
- 1 cup of grated parmesan cheese
- ½ stick of butter

In a saucepan, melt butter slowly and add half & half and cheese. Stir with whisk until boiling. Simmer until thickened and toss with pasta.

Pasta Greca

- 2-3 Red bell peppers
- 1 bag of spinach
- 2 tsp. of chopped garlic
- 1 small container of feta cheese
- ½ cup of black olives
- 1 lb. of pasta
- Olive oil

Sauté olive oil and garlic. Add peppers until tender. Add spinach until cooked. Toss mixture with cooked pasta. Garnish with cheese and olives.

Pizelles

- 1 dozen eggs
- 2 cups of oil or margarine (melted and cooled)
- 3 cups of sugar
- 8 cups of flour
- 4 tsp. of baking powder
- Lemon, orange, vanilla and anise extracts.

Grease electric pizelle iron and pre-heat. Melt margarine and let cool. Beat eggs and sugar. Gradually add extracts to taste. Add baking powder and mix well. Gradually add flour until well blended. Mix in melted margarine. Drop by teaspoonful into pizelle iron. Cook until desired golden brown.

<u>**Erica Hollabaugh – Alba's Granddaughter**</u>

Pizza Baked Ziti

- 1 lb. of Ziti
- 1 jar of sauce
- 1package of pepperoni

- 1 lb. of mozzarella cheese
- Parmesan cheese – grated

Preheat oven to 400 degrees. Cook pasta as directed. Cover with choice of sauce. Spread mozzarella cheese over pasta. Top with desired amount of pepperoni and grated cheese. Bake for 20-25 minutes or until bubbling and cheese has melted.

Crock Pot Roast

- 1 roast (cut of choice)
- 1 whole onion
- ½ cup of water
- Lemon pepper, garlic salt, pepper
- Soy sauce
- Worcestershire sauce

Place roast and water into crock-pot. Cover with soy and Worcestershire sauces. Sprinkle on all spices. Cook on high for four hours or on low for six to eight hours. Shred with fork.

Chapter Four

Alba's Childhood War Experience

The youngest of nine children, Alba DiGenova was born in 1934 in Sulmona, Italy (Abruzzo). Her parents, Cosimo and Lucia DiGenova, and her elder three brothers and sisters, suffered through the pains of war and occupation, which still live vividly in their recollections.

Italy had surrendered its part during World War II and the Germans were quick to occupy Alba's hometown of Sulmona. Not only was the city occupied, but many homes, including Alba's, were staffed with German soldiers. The Germans stationed their military shoemaker and tailor in the DiGenova home and the German commander took up residence two doors down.

Alba distinctly remembers the family having to hide her brothers in the home's attic for fear that the Germans would take them for endless months of hard labor in their notorious labor battalions. The battalions would repair war torn roads and remove snow for the advance of the advancing German army. Thus, the family kept their sons hidden for over a year. A chore made difficult with Germans living in the home and in the near vicinity.

As an eight year-old child, Alba was given the duties as the lookout when the family snuck food and water to the boys. She would also play the same role in order to have them go to the bathroom and she assisted in the task of hiding the ladder, which led to the attic.

As time went on, the Germans soldiers living in the home would join the family around the fire on cold days. They also had families suffering in Germany and they sympathized with their host's situation. Eventually, the family befriended the two soldiers stationed in their home and, in turn, the soldiers never reported the existence of the DiGenova boys hiding in the house.

Due to the German occupation of Sulmona, American planes would often bomb the city. They had established air bases in Foggia and LaPuglia, which gave them easy access to the region. The roar of the planes sent chills through young Alba as the family scrambled to close all lights in the home, leaving only the fireplace active for warmth. The air raid alarms would soon sound and if the lights were not turned off, German soldiers trying to protect their position from the planes, would actually shoot out the lights.

As the planes came closer, the Italian citizens would run from their homes and directly to their fields of crops, which would provide them better protection from explosions and falling debris. Alba remembers her father racing into the fields with food rations that he had taken from the Italian military barracks. He dispensed the food to his neighbors in the fields.

Fighter planes would often swoop down and strafe German Jeeps that scrambled through the city and many were destroyed right in front of the DiGenova home. The war presented daily hazards for Alba and her family. In the fields one day, a German Jeep passed on the nearest road and was soon attacked by fighter planes. A barrage of bullets narrowly missed Alba, who was in the field assisting her family. The Jeep was destroyed right before her.

Food was also scarce in occupied Italy, as the Germans controlled the food supply. Commerce did not exist to sell to the public under the occupation. The Germans fed their soldiers first and had little concern whether the civilians were well fed. The DiGenova had to hide the little food that they had or else the Germans would take it. They had already taken their chickens, pig and stash of potatoes, thus the family resorted to hiding rice and beans in an old chicken coop. Alba, being the smallest, was given the task of sliding through the small door to retrieve the rice and beans for a family meal. They would also pick dandelions and cook them as a vegetable. They also had a barrel of wine hidden below their floorboards. This was the extent of their food supply until the Germans allowed one slice of bread to each citizen, per day.

Alba rationed her food with the rest of the family. She, being the smallest, was also given the smallest portions, which she accepted. She recalls one day when her fortunes turned for a moment. It was a snowy day and the snow accumulated heavily while Alba played in front of her house. The schools were closed during the height of the German occupation and Alba missed six-months of schooling. With little to do, she wandered in the snow until she noticed a German soldier passing her front gate. She glanced up and noticed that the solider was reaching in his pocket. The soldier paused and threw her a handful of candy, which was the ultimate treat.

Based on these experiences...food has always been special for Alba. Appreciate what you have and enjoy good times with good food.

"Volete mangiare bene, mangia Abruzzese"

Chapter Five

Sulmona – A True Italian City – Alba's Hometown

Hemmed in by mountains and sitting comfortably in a lush valley, Sulmona is a prosperous small city with a charming medieval core. Sulmona has various piazzas, churches and palaces of historical and tourist interest. Some of these include:

- Piazza Garibaldi is the main piazza, which includes a span of Gothic, 12th century Roman aqueducts and a large baroque era fountain at its center. This is the center of town and the square hosts a market twice a week on Wednesdays and Saturdays. The piazza is also famous for two tourist-attracting events. The Madonna che Scappa in Piazza (Easter ceremony) involves a procession of a statue of the Madonna, whose bearers race across the piazza to meet the statue of the resurrected Christ. Every summer, A Palio style medieval festival and horse race, known as Giostra Cavalleresca, takes place in the piazza.
- Piazza XX Settembre, another of the main squares of the city, includes a bronze statue of the Roman poet Ovid. Ovid was born in Sulmona and many credit him with writing the first love poems and helping to create the St. Valentine's Day holiday.
- Palazzo Annunziata-A Palace containing an excellent museum depicting the Roman history of the city, as well as various artifacts.
- Cattedrale di San Panfilo is the city's primary cathedral and sits on the northwest side of the old city and was built on the site of a Roman temple. It contains a crypt, which retains its Romanesque appearance despite the 18th Century renovation of the main church.
- Chiesa della St. Annuziata – A baroque church which includes a fine example of architecture, an ornate interior and bell tower.
- Corso Ovidio-The city's main thoroughfare that connects the cathedrals and the major piazzas and is also lined by elegant covered arcades, shops, cafes, and parks. The road is closed nightly to traffic, allowing for leisurely strolls by pedestrians.

The city also has several other historical palaces: Palazzo Meliorati, Palace Sanità, Palazzo Tabassi, Palazzo Sardi. A visit to Sulmona can start through one of its ancient doors, one of which is of Roman age- Porta Romana. This ancient door will lead you towards the churches of Saint Filippo Neri and Saint Maria della Tomba in the Plebiscito square.

Other churches certainly worth visiting include San Francesco delle Scarpe, which was constructed in the 13th century and San Panfilo, an 11th century cathedral. Much of Sulmona's modern wealth is based on the production of confetti, the sugar-coated almonds presented to guests at Italian weddings and a number of other events (also known as Jordan Almonds). There is also a small, but burgeoning jewelry industry.

This once walled city also has remnants of ruins just outside of its gates. Vestiges of an amphitheater, a theatre, and thermae exist at the foot of the Monte Morrone, as are some ruins of masonry buildings, probably belonging to a Roman villa, traditionally believed to be of Ovidio Nasone (Ovid), Italy's most famous ancient Latin poet (Amores and Metamorphoses) – circa 43 b.c. Nearby is an excellent Roman-period archaeological site, which is a temple dedicated to Ercole Curino, also known as the god Zeus. Sulmona also has a mountainside hermitage said to be Eremo di Sant'Onofrio. This location gave shelter to the only outgoing Pope of history: Celestino V, known as the "Pope of the great refusal"-cited by Dante in the Divina Commedia. Sulmona was also the home of Pope Innocenzo VII.

Bibliography

Italy Central – iUniverse
La Terra dei Peligrini – Edzizioni Amaltea
L'Abruzzo-Edzioni Pama Graphicolor
Sulmona Ieri – Mattiocco
Wikipedia
Various websites

About the Author

Rock DiLisio's other books include Italy Central, American Advance, Firings From the Fox Hole and Archaeology In-Brief. In addition, his fictional series includes Night in the Galaxies, Three Kings of Casablanca, Stone of the Sahara, Palace of the Pharaoh and Sherlock Holmes: Mysteries of the Victorian Era. His work has also appeared in various magazines, newspapers and periodicals.

Made in the USA
Middletown, DE
27 November 2017